CW01080251

THE DESECRATION OF TREES

Lotte Kramer

THE DESECRATION OF TREES

Lotte Kramer

HIPPOPOTAMUS PRESS

ACKNOWLEDGEMENTS are due to the editors of the following magazines, periodicals and anthologies.

Acumen, Agenda, Ambit, AJR Information, Ariel (Canada), *The Christian Science Monitor* (U.S.A.), *Chapman, Country Life, Cyphers* (Eire), *Encounter, European Judaism Grand Piano, The Green Book, The Jewish Chronicle, The Jewish Quarterly, Leamington Poetry Society No. 4, Literary Review, The Month, The Observer, Other Poetry, Outposts Poetry Quarterly, PEN New Poetry 11, The P.E.N., PEN INTERNATIONAL, Poetry Canada Review* (Canada), *Poetry Durham, Proof, The Rialto, 'Shades of Green' Editor: Anne Harvey (Julia MacCrea), New Spokes, Stand, Ver Poets, The Wiener Library. 'In the Gold of the Flesh'* (Women's Press)

The Hippopotamus Press gratefully acknowledges the financial assistance of the Arts Council

First published 1994 by
HIPPOPOTAMUS PRESS
22, Whitewell Road, Frome, Somerset

© Lotte Kramer 1994

British Library Cataloguing in Publication Data.
A catalogue record for this book is available from the British Library

ISBN 0 904179 58 3 Cloth
ISBN 0 904179 54 0 Pbk

Ten copies of the cloth edition have been numbered and signed by the author

Cover photograph: Frederic Kramer

Printed in Great Britain by
Latimer Trend & Company Ltd, Plymouth, Devon

CONTENTS

IV VERSIONS AND TRANSLATIONS

Three versions from Rilke

For F.K.

'Sag ihm Dinge. Er wird staunender stehn;'
Rainer Maria Rilke (9th Elegy)

I

KADDISH

Thirty years on:
The wall unbricks itself
And look by look a childhood's
Rawness stands and turns:
"Confront me Now!"

Forty years on:
The named, the nameless queue
And walk their histories,
Demand a chronicle:
"Remember us!"

Fifty years on:
Not late, not loud, the trumpet
Weeps this jubilee,
The skeletons return:
Sad hieroglyphs.

OXFORD, 1940s

Then I was "Mother's Help—Lady's Companion",
A teen-age girl in love with fantasies
Walking the wartime Oxford streets and lanes.

The colleges were locked facades to me
Quite out of bounds with military use
But still regarded with romantic awe

As territories one day to be explored
By one who'd shed the enemy alien skin.
Meanwhile there were the books—some treasured

Second-hand, picked up at Blackwell's for a song.
An early Schnitzler with the spine in shreds
And hinted sex in dashes worming through

To savour secretly. Before permissiveness.
Long, lonely afternoons up Shotover,
The hill that took me past an empty church

I sometimes entered, praying in my search
For something new and weatherproof
But never found. Years looking for a clue.

A cleric gave a lecture, gaunt, severe,
On faith, a Puritan of sorts, a Scot
Who sent me down a draughty corridor

A mile or two. Not very far. 'Macbeth'
Came to the theatre and filled my head,
My bones and bloodstream ever since, the breath

Of witches stoking up my words. A flame
As permanent as air. And British
Restaurants would earn their wholesome name

With calories that lined my ribs. U.S.
Canteens were treasure troves that sometimes
Spilled their gems. And war was somewhere else.

COFFEE GRINDING

Grinding the coffee in my moulinex
The beans explode their old aroma here.
It clears the ashes out of sleep.

My mind returns to kitchens where I played:
I see our maid, broad on a stool, machine
Placed firmly between thighs:

She wheels the scent with comfortable arms
And sings of love in tune to grating knives.
A reassurance grinds.

I am reminded of another scene:
There, in the synagogue my mother stands
All day to fast and pray;

To keep her from a faintness now I bring
Some coffee finely ground, wafting a strength
Into her silent fears.

THE NON-EMIGRANT (*my father in Nazi Germany*)

He left the application forms
Hidden inside his desk and missed
His quota for the U.S.A.

He thought he'd stay and wait and stare
The madness out. It could not last.
He would not emigrate, not lose

His home, his language and his ground.
Beside his armchair sat a pile
Of books; the smoke from his cigar

Fenced comfort with a yellow screen.
His daily walk was all he'd need,
He thought. Abroad was where he'd been.

LOVE LETTERS

Alone at home one afternoon
I found them in my father's desk.
A bolted fortress, as a rule—
But now a drawer yielded,
There they lay, ribboned
And stacked in one elaborate box:
Letters my parents had received
Before their marriage.

Strange sympathy I felt
For that young Christian girl
His mother disapproved of—
For many years her lines
Had burnt and cradled him.
Hers were the only ones he'd kept.

But on my mother's side
A pot-pourri of males:
Some officers in trenches
Shimmering with her praises
Written in muddy misery.
Another she'd made eyes at
From a theatre box;
One, a Black Forest holiday friend
Who even called her 'bride'—
All pleading on their paper knees!

Like pickles they had been preserved
Inside this occult box
Not seeing daylight much,
Not for a daughter's eyes.

RED WALLPAPER

You choose red paper for your living room.
"How dark and claustrophobic" I remark
But then regret. Because I see the place
Where as a child I'd sit and fight with food,
Despite my father's warning rock my chair
Until it topples over—then a scene.

The red damask stared ogres from the walls
And sinister, the carved oak furniture
Condoned my punishment.—Now, when your daughter
Picks at meals and you get angry, shout—
The nightmare train of 'red' transports me back
To fashions that assert their elegance
With fear. Give me a white-washed dining room
Instead of walls that nail you down and bleed.

EQUUS POWER

Lorries torturing the tarmac
Intent on discharging
Their dubious commodities

Remind me of the hot day
When arriving home from school
I met a dark mass of horse

Spreadeagled in the yard's doorway.
His sad eye in his half-turned head,
His collapsed rump damp on cobbles,

The cart across the pavement
Stacked tall with crates of bottles
That have nowhere to go.

Men tried to lift him up
But sent me away—
Not to hear or witness

That mutual futility
Pointing the afternoon
To a bullet's answer.

LENA, our maid

She anchored all my needs
In her solidity,
A cross pleat on her brow.

Between her household chores
She'd rush with me to school,
Her rough hands square with love.

Devout, she made me kneel
On crowded pavement slabs
To watch the bishop pass

Under his baldachin
Intoning Latin chant,
The incense cloud above.

At the stone kitchen sink,
Her yeasty body's shrine,
She'd stand and strip-wash clean,

Then outings into town,
To dark room secrecy
Where she collected hope

From a clairvoyant's words
Behind a curtain fall,
Her love-life's counterpoint.

A butcher boy appeared
And many nights they sighed
On mother's lounge settee

While I pretended sleep
Two doors away. She got
Her man and left. I cried.

Her home two basement rooms
Where she would lie in wait
With plates of chips, the food

I loved, spoiling my lunch.
But still I hear her screams
Up in my room, two floors

Above her flat, when she
Gave birth to her huge son
Her second child, she said.

'WIENER BLUT'

I can still hear it,
The thin waltz on the hand-wound
Gramophone in the long, baroque ball-room,
The glittering horse-shoe table
Shrouded in white,

The bride and bridegroom
Pinned to the centre like jewels
Surrounded by clusters of uncles and aunts,
A tall cousin putting on records
With a distracting grin,

And all eyes on me
In a pink tulle ballet dress
Dancing to the music and getting lost
On the geometry of the Persian carpet
When 'Wiener Blut'

Decreed its own rhythm
And I was crisscrossing another
The inevitable round of the waltz eluding
My well-rehearsed steps
To my nightmare shame.

PUBERTY

The Rhineland heat hung heavy in the street.
Across the road with windows open wide
The opera singer practised his great roles.

Framed in his room's own shadow distanced him,
His naked torso white—as I, half-grown,
Watched him in safety from my recessed dark.

One day he fixed my eyes with his, brought voice
And hands together in a plea, unnerved
Me with his begging aria of love.

And when he motioned me to strip as well
I stepped back terrified in secret shock,
Excited and yet unable to leave.

I told no one. We never spoke. He'd haunt
All summer. When I saw him laugh with women
In the street I'd look away and flee.

10TH NOVEMBER 1938 (Kristallnacht)

You evoke eloquent images,
Spokesmen for the throttled, the fear-bruised,
But you cannot hear the stark dawn-bell
Nor see the meagre groups of children, afraid.

The early, tapped telephone warning:
'Don't leave the house, the school is burning!'
The furtive attic floor trembling with
Slap-happy sticks that splinter safety and home.

You don't feel my father's hidden tread
In woods while the thicket's cancer grew
Nor his secret return whispering
Family shadows, the vanished ones that day.

You cannot build crosses with your tongue,
So rich and round, for the precision
Of the operation; wear the thorns
Of ice that walk with anonymous ashes

Because the useless shot in Paris
Burst a man's heart—and his mother's also.

Note: a young Polish Jew shot a German official
which triggered off the well-prepared pogrom.

AT BURGHLEY HOUSE

We walk here
Where each tree and shrub
Is a planned cypher
In Capability Brown's charter;
Where Englishness
And Tudor stone surround us
And pale sun whitens
Our footprints in the grass.
Your questions
Curl with American vowels
As they should after all those years
Since we walked along the Rhine
On a November day
Bright with dread and ashes
When flames had taken
Our holiest places.
Overnight
We had learnt the language
Of terror, but still could walk
Carelessly, as children will,
By that river that shone.

THE LADDER

Today she came,
The lady of good works,
To talk of faith
Behind her coffee cup,
To strum the keys
Of her utopian chord.

"They did not die in vain,
Those children in the cattle trucks,
You'll see their spirit rise
And gather peace throughout the world."

And goodness shone like butter
On her face and oiled
Her hot-line ladder to the sky
And who am I
Here, on the lowest rung?

JET-LAG

Back in the village street
The thatch of the old house
Is sodden black with rain,
A mattress path of leaves
Supports me underfoot
As jet-lagged I retain
Those giants of New York
Where sunlight awed their shapes
Doubled in Hudson's face.

My fog-lined limbs and brain
Refuse their morning tread.
I still connect that hill
That crowns Manhattan's speed
With all those transplant stones:
The 'Cloisters' quiet spell,
And echo chapels sit
High on the tallest towers
Downtown where markets crash.

But meeting you again
I hugged my childhood hours,
And looking like our mothers
We talked of Europe, home,
And wondered at our sons:
Yours with athletic build,
A new-world muscle walk,
Mine with my father's eyes
Holding our jet-lagged past.

BILINGUAL

When you speak German
The Rhineland opens its watery gates,
Lets in strong currents of thought.
Sentences sit on shores teeming
With certainties. You cross bridges
To travel many lifetimes
Of a captive's continent.

When you speak English
The hesitant earth softens your vowels.
The sea—never far away—explores
Your words with liquid memory.
You are an apprentice again and skill
Is belief you can't quite master
In your adoptive island.

Myself, I'm unsure
In both languages. One, with mothering
Genes, at once close and foreign
After much unuse. Near in poetry.
The other, a constant love affair
Still unfulfilled, a warm
Shoulder to touch.

SECOND THOUGHTS

The day
I sold some family silver
At first I felt no regret;
But then
The gaps in drawers, cupboards,
Stared back with pity and awe.
There began
The lost clutter and dance
Of salvers, bowls, spoons.
I knew it
As a kind of homesickness,
That permanent claw in the blood,
But also
As freedom from possessions,
As pleasure at parting
From things
That told and heavied the heart
With a tyrant's mirror.

LAMENT AND CELEBRATION
i.m. Greta Berdolt

You now
Under a blanket of flowers
Diminish
My childhood's mirror:

Though I stood
In the yard of the old house
Looking up
To your terrace of summer,
Your voice
Of Schubert's 'Lindenbaum'
Cutting the bark
Of the afternoon's quiet;
I have walked
Past wine-soaked cellars
Hearing the organ
You played in St. Stefan's.

At nightfall
You taught me to see
Fairytale castles
In the fire's landscape;
Midsummer
In a midnight park
You showed me
Pin-lights of glow-worms.
Through streets of terror
You came as night's shadow
Giving new names
To courage and love.

Again the heat
In the leafstill forest,
The dominant river
We can swim in no longer.
Your presence
In your garden's coolness,
A roof of trees
In secret corners
After the spade's earthfall.

BARRICADES

She is wailing in the archaic
German of her childhood
Across continents of cinders
Unthought of by doctors and nurses.

In her long-ago house
She sends us down to the cellar
Through a coal-dark door
To fetch a bottle of lemonade.

She is waiting with certainty
For her dead husband's arrival
But weeps because 'too many
Stones on the path—
              he can't cross the stones.'

Her room is my prison.
My shame is my fear
Of her plundered world
I refuse to enter.

THE DESECRATION OF TREES
(*in appreciation of Peter Handke's 'ACROSS'*)

Someone, now well past middle-age, white-haired,
Has painted swastikas on trees. So says
The poet-writer in his book. Fiction and
Fact, maybe, though it has followed me for days

And the spontaneous murder it provoked.
What better signature of brain-washed, sick
Disciples still alive and star-struck
By that false elixir of a decade?

I look about me, see the tendrils flare,
That crooked emblem bore through brain and sleep.
The scapegoat has two thousand lives. We weep,
We try to tie a knot in time, prepare

To praise and tell our children's children of
The constant Good—a mushroom crime of love.

THEFT

This summer was the shortest I remember.
That season's paucity prepares no winter.

So we complain until we read about
That chimney sweep who stands in Leningrad,

A shadow of himself, a scientist
Whose words hardly accuse, only explain:

'I know now that they've stolen my life.'
There is no summer in his strangled year.

Ilya Shatakovsky, former scientist, now chimney sweep.

II

BLACK FOREST SONNETS

I
The Yugoslav waiter—the first wrong sounds
In this old house where the Black Forest creeps
To the door, meadows are littered with mounds
Of wild flowers, a blanket of needles keeps

The roots warm and the sun shadows each tall
Tree trunk with a collage of textured earth
Colours. Still the same, out there, the shrill call
Of a hawk in the quiet woods, the slow breath

Of cows in the valley, the farmer's soft
Sing-song speech I imbibed with my first milk;
The lake's water as gentle. Nothing left
Unremembered. Only uneasy talk

Of the hotel's bankruptcy, of this, the last
Summer by the church-clock's quarterly blast.

II
The dark grit of wild bilberries grates
In my mouth, picked where moss and grasses stand
Thick like shampooed heads of hair, in pleats
Among tree trunks. Some firs dead with acid

Rain. But forest still saga-deep, a pulpit
For myths and histories. A sudden stone
And cross tell of a man's murder, his throat
Cut in 1810 for eleven Gulden.

Today we walk in summer air as mild
As butter. Foxgloves high between heather
And raspberries sweeter than remembered.
A red squirrel shoots up a tree and here,

A surprise lizard dead, or pretend dead
On the path, stretched flat and grey as old lead.

III
In this Caspar David Friedrich landscape
Valleys are surprise gifts that delight,
Widen our bonus freedom and escape.
Peaks add their own discoveries; the last

Light wallows in the sky, views concentrate
The distance beyond frontiers. Here wars
Have left a cross or a grave where someone's fate
Was shattered on a hill, down there where cars

Rush by the edge of forests. Always
Memorials, inscriptions, to make you halt
Your steps and plant a quiet thought in the place.
At night the darkness penetrates like salt

In hot soup. The deer collect the silence
Safe now from the day's precarious sentence.

IV
In the Schlosspark someone stole our camera.
The man in the kiosk is sure the thief
Won't go to heaven. But interior
Of castle is light baroque with a brief

Joyful period of rococo. The taste
Of the princess was immaculate. Outside
The supposed source of the Danube encased
In railings and a small pond. Much is restored

And rebuilt in this town since the last war.
In the station restaurant a Bertold
Brecht character glares at his glass of beer
And flies riot all over the place. Old

Girlie magazines and others with Princess
Di on the cover stare out among the mess.

V

After the night's rain the forest dripping
Warm showers, clear sprays on squelching grass.
Wind warns in the trees its distant wailing.
Big puddles in the red sand soil like glass

With copper backing, puncture the lane.
Everywhere are tall stacks of logs prepared
For winter. Wood: the currency, the brain
Of this region. Pine, so dark and rigid,

Lording it above all others in these
Dense hills, but soft and light when at home.
Albino innocence in its stripped use.
How deceptive the Black Forest name

When encountered in cupboards, tables, chairs,
The smell and crackle of wood-burning flares.

VI

At the forest Gasthaus the landlady
Tells us of the downfall of the local
Wealthy family. How all the money
Had been grabbed by the son-in-law, his final

Escape with his girl-friend. How the pampered
Wife had to face auction of their great house
Alone. How her old widowed mother had
Cried in the forest so loud that others

Could hear her. Everyone saw it coming
A mile off. And old grandfather so proud
Years ago, he wouldn't allow a thing
To spoil the peace of the village. No crowd

Ever. He wouldn't permit the railway
With its noise into our horse-drawn valley!

WEISSENSEE

I *Morning*

A storm in the night left meadow and wood
Sodden as washing. Clouds are settled
Featherbeds. Yesterday a rabbit dead
And stretched white on a soft hill. Flies fed

On his fur. We stared and questioned. No blood.
His brown companion hopping about him
A funeral rite, perplexed. We saw sad
Lines on his flapping face. Or a whim

Of our fancy, perhaps. Today no corpse
But wild mint profuse at the waterfall,
Strong scent among flowers and raindrops
As we goose-stepped our way along the wall

Of sheerness. Then in the forest the path
Knotted with roots. No slippery aftermath.

II *Evening*

Aspen leaves like stitched-on butterflies
Demand our eyes; high aircraft vapour
Slings an arrow trail dividing skies
From beyond the mountain tops further
And further against blue. The lake now
At its most tranquil with the odd small
Boat where a toy man stands fishing. How
Near we are to perfection where tall
Grasses and sedge cull their strength in wind
And meadows hoard waves that are static
By the edge of the wood. Here the mind
Cannot curl its barbed wire mesh of sick
Sorceries; is hijacked by a seedling
Of late evening sun, almost willing.

III *Night*
A porcelain wind on the dark lake at night
Away from the crush of the floodlit shore
And bodies dancing to music irate
With the wrong rhythm. We submit more and more

To liquid blackness dotted with stars
And the slow movement of the boat inside
A huge sky. Until—a gush, a fall, the scars
Of fireworks rising and bending, a ride

Of colour and flame linking dark with dark
In explosions. Almost against our will
We adore that fusion: a bulwark
Of living where noise must marry the still

Elements, and with our 'Ohs' and 'Ahs'
Be part and parcel of the ransacked glass.

ARRAN POEMS

1 *Trekking*

On the way to the waterfall
We met a lost sheep
Fanfaring his aloneness
Through moss and bracken.
Somehow he had crossed
The unquiet river
Where boulders bridge
Their quarried path.
He looked at us with shocked eyes
And rushed into no-man's-land
As we stood helpless
Bog-weary in a dug-out of swamp.
Later we heard his cries again
Still hoarse in knolls of heather
Haunting us home.

2 *Rain*

Rain initials this island
Inch by inch.
It signs each tree and flower,
Each pebble on the sea-hungry shore
Where yesterday's sun had bleached
A bench on the grass.
Today it sits there nameless and washed.
The hills are smudges
Whispering under grey wool,
Hardly alive.
A blue boat ducks
Under the relentless signature.

3 *Lamlash Bay opposite Holy Isle*

To let this bay caress you in your veins,
To be a central island set in light,
To look across the misted hills where sight
Is interrupted by the rocks, to let
The sea collect your every thought and breath:
You would be homeless here at home at last,
You would be nameless in this island's name.

4 *The Tide*

Every time
The bay is bandaged
By the sea
Covering wounded rocks,
Sand and grass.
Like big sores
They reveal themselves
When the tide goes out.
Then we walk
In lanes of lesions
Picking our way
Through healing answers.

III

III

NOT FLOWERS BUT STONES

Not flowers but stones
We bring to our graves.
Perhaps to build
An edifice of permanence
So that in death
The wandering myth
Might cease, console
The earth with kith and kin
Of its own pseudonym.
The named and nameless
Bloom and sing
In spells of stones.

FAR FROM HERE

The terror of this day is far from here.
We hold our breath, switch on the radio voice
And wait for miracles, imagine fear,

The heat and stench in airless atmosphere
Caught on that indexed flight without a choice;
The terror of this day is far from here.

To write of horror doesn't bring it near.
Words only pave the distance with their noise
And wait for miracles, imagine fear.

A new spring cloaks the trees, I see it leer
Between the grasses creeping to the house.
The terror of this day is far from here.

The North wind orphans cobwebs, covets hair
In fierce hostility; we guard our eyes
And wait for miracles, imagine fear.

For yet another summer, a whole year
We are as ants purloining earth and space.
The terror of this day is far from here,
We wait for miracles, imagine fear.

TWO WOMEN IN ROUEN

Some towns have corners that cry out the names
Of ghosts, and so in Rouen where two women
Followed me: that girl holding her sword is
Everywhere, her voices whispering high
And low, in market halls, in gabled streets,
In squares of stone that shine flamboyant
With success and age, and in that final
Newness of one church: a ship embedded
With its roof aflame spiking the sky
In metal scales of armour. And where
The half-moon pews of polished wood still
Hear her judgment, under the rounded vault
And sunlit side of coloured glass, she sings—
Her stake outside a tall, demanding cross.

Another, much more quiet and subdued
Although her woman's passion fills the streets
Where she had travelled in a coach or walks
In ecstasy and grief; where with her anxious
Eyes she tries to lunge at love inside
A dark cathedral's nave, in dusty
Small hotels by harbour walls until
Her final loneliness turns to despair.
As real and tragic as that other one
She feeds on flames of her too human needs.

SPRING IN PROVENCE

Even the birds have double summer time
In this rich region where the stumps of vines
Stand regimented in dark knots. Here Greece

And Rome have left their massive mark, from Africa
Some heavy footprints penetrate the earth:
Orange with light it still resounds their names.

And Jews—at Carpentras they payed their dues
To Popes at nearby Avignon to build
Their tiny heaven saved from Spain, still now

They gather there, in this carved house, to pray.
The hills are pricked with scrub and gorse in bloom
Like yellow stars that melted in the sun.

And further South, near Arles, you see van Gogh's
Great swirl of paint do justice to the land,
You feel the mistral's madness take your hair

To tune the rondo of his cypress trees.
But not one lonely house or stone remains
That he could call his home or refuge there.

'Le pont de Langlois' is a replica.
Yet still he strides into the fields with us
Under those energetic clouds and skies.

MASKS

In this city of masks,
Owl-eyed and golden
Or bird-beaked and white,
Our waiter's face
Is a fitting example:
When he gives his advice
Not to eat salad with sea-bass
His eyes horse-gleam
Superiority and sadness
In his long, lean visage.

Aschenbach's ghost
Sways through the lanes
Where heels click and echo,
Canals grow black
As gondolas glide by,
An elderly tenor
'Solo Mios' with 'Bravo'
Applauding from bridges;
The will of reflections
Usurping the night.

From Browning's palace,
Heavy with chandeliers,
We step out to smells
Of decay and sea-breeze
And much-painted views.
Here literature strengthens
Reality; or will they threaten
Our unprinted eyes:
Those Shylocks, Tadzios,
Aschenbachs?

CLOSING TIME

In Ermine Street
We saw Time close in
On itself when a black
Clockface of Now
Stared out from an old
Church tower.
It stood in a tide of grass
Unable to fathom
Our rush to the sea.

FLAG FEN

"This is where England used to end"
He pointed to the line of trees,
    "Where you stand now, a Roman road
    Was laid on water, feeding skies."

Crows overhead. A young owl learns
To hunt the sun, the reclaimed land
Lies black and silted in these Fens
Where ancient wood preserved in bog
Is currency to purchase lives.

We troop along the site and freeze
As air sings harshly 'water, wind,
Water and wind' in constant canons.
New spring is hinting in the grass.

Flag Fen is a bronze-age site near Peterborough

RESEARCH IN CROWLAND AND PEAKIRK
(for Shirley Toulson)

The fen-light bleached the day
As we approached the abbey's
Site, watched Guthlac's stone
Become a sun-licked apricot.

And later, in the nun's large smile,
You found the confirmation
That you need, to speak of Pega's
Journey through the fens.

There we unlocked the church
And saw the stone, grey and too
Ordinary, it seemed, to hold
That sister's heart returned from Rome.

Two fenland villages affirmed
And equalled silence on that day
With whole devotion centuries ago,
Two island witnesses.

DISUSED RAILWAY LINE

Rusting and bereaved
Of the weight of wheels
The celibate line
Ladders the horizon.

Crows black-button
The grass at intervals
Depressing frost
That has sugared its blades.

We follow this flat
Staircase, aware
Of dead journeys
To destinations

Crumbling with unuse.
We negotiate gaps
In a museum of steam
Painting the sky white

As wildflowers recover
Hesitant faces
In sooty soil
Remembering their roots.

PAINTING UNDER THE BRIDGE

For a long time she looks
At the sepia eye of the river
Demanding knowledge,
And the slow maze of ripples
Tells of other encounters
Trundling their waters downstream.
Islands are lying in wait,

Inlets and looping arms
Trying to hold on to the odd
Handful of pleasure; some
Sedge and watermeadows
Succeed for a season
And bulrushes gossip
Their flatteries to the wind.

But history will repeat
Its delusions, seeping
Blind, muddy movements
Into tubes of paint until
Decisions giddy the canvas
With confetti of sunlight
Defying the river's laughter.

I.M. RITZ CINEMA

The Bauhaus Ritz is dead.
The red-brick elephant
Sits empty in the city street,
His musty smells no longer brush
The heat of make-belief.
All's withered in his dusty plush.

We mourn this loss of meeting place
That now will turn to concrete, glass,
To swell the coffers of the town
And in its icy centre holds
No ivory lights that nightly pass,
No warmth where queues of arteries cross.

AT POOLE'S CAVERN, Derbyshire

Now duck your head
And step inside the darkest hill,
The cave where rivers start,
Where water sculpts
More mysteries and shapes
Than man can contemplate.
Walk gingerly and see:
The forest calcified,
The columns guarding
Secret passages,
The hollow spears above
Descend from boulders;
The shades of half-tones
Leering grey to blue
Surprised by orange, chalk;
And even stars will glisten
As you hear millennia grow
In single waterdrops.
But all the time the chill
Invades you, dampness
Skins your face and hair,
You turn and touch your way
Back to escape, greedy
For light's horizon.

LETTER OPENER

This ivory dagger
Is good to hold
By its grip of chased silver.

Three generations
Have twisted this point
In discreet discoveries;

A servant of Sesame
For joy and tragedy
For everyday boredom,

But most appealing
In its passive state:
An unageing bone

With patina echoes
Telling flat tales
Of crusader words.

SPRING CLEANING

I take the books down, one by one,
A yearly ritual meeting point,
And dust them carefully, each spine

A recognition sometimes met
With half-forgotten joy, sometimes
A frayed familiar like a pet

Much handled and aglow with use.
I pile them on the floor aware
Of hoarding far too many: those

That have outlived their youthful fire
And company, that escapade
Of first surrender, now a bore.

But though I curse their bulk and greed
I can't discard them yet; something
That charts myself lies there, a load

Of stepping stones. Who knows how long
The Sisyphus in me will heave
For the great line, for the new song,

Catching the old words in my sleeve?

TOKEN

A replica, a jug, an ornament.
You brought it from your travels years ago.
I put it safely behind wood and glass

And then you went abroad, left early friends
For more demanding continents. I broke
The thing today, caught in my hasty sleeve

I had to watch it fall and shatter
On the floor, the shards beyond repair.
And as I gather up the fragments,

As I sweep corrupted time into our
Furnished past, I know I still must find
A token gift in your sparse letters now.

HER SILENCE

He turned her picture to the wall.
He could not bear to see her face.
Her eyes would burn him, so he feared,
And turned her round to scorch the wall.

But in his head she'd call and call
And fill his orphaned hands with waste.
The years were solid sounds of grief
Because he heard her call and call.

Yet in that room one day the light
Defended death, forced him to find
Her oval smile, her knotted hair,
Her silence in that room's new light.

WHITENESS

Moments of knowledge
Surround her pale eyes,
Her snow hair.

She walks with caution
Testing the ground
With each step.

But sorrow is absent.
Only her skin sighs,
Her bones lament.

She has a pact with water.
With her cold Baltic
Embalming her each year,

With her daylight summer
That floods her body's winter
Clean with whiteness.

BACKBONE

"The thing is: you've become invisible—
At parties or when walking down the street
No one will stop and stare, look back and tell
With eyes his admiration. A defeat

Of sorts. I've noticed it as years collapse
My face, pucker my skin and thin my hair.
But I don't mind. Only regret my hips
Are bolshy, obdurate with pain and wear.

Once I could hold an audience from the stage,
Assert a spell with eyes and voice and smile
Such sweetness as would multiply the rage
Of stars! Now, as the mirror charts each mile,

Conjures up ghosts of friends that trod the boards,
My time is trapped in vertebrae of words."

REUNION

They pick up each other's gestures
From ageing bodies,
Outline of noses and chins,

Recognize eyes.
Recall the code of a sentence
Or scraps of poetry;

Mad summers in Kent
Carrying wreaths of hops
From village to village

Their scent preaching.
Today, in a room,
In the centre of England,

They flaunt the trunk of their lives
But dwell on the peak
Of that pyramid youth.

ACCESSIONING, Peterborough Museum

"Look at his 1914 army boots!"
Caked with his garden mud they now perch
On the basement table, stiff like some roots
Of stone. A carved van Gogh ready to march

Off to the Somme. Or would they rather churn
Themselves in dirt, tread fen-soil foot on spade,
Not wait here, dusty for computer terms,
Be wrapped in tissue paper, boxed and named

As artefacts?—We sort his library:
Philosophy and history, literature
Too, and true to his moustache and stature
His German language bristled. But not one tee

Prepared us for those scripted cookery books
With 'Mother' at the top of jams and cakes.

IN LIMBO (Peterborough Museum)

The basement hugs
A parade of astonishments:

A lop-side Roman altar
Nudging a tomato pillar-box,

Flints and stone-tools
Laid out on long tables,

Labelled, polished like necklaces
Inviting touch,

Returning in the blotched mirror
Of elegant ancestry.

Artefacts and utilities,
Each century spits them out

Like cherry stones, for us to finger,
Stroke tenderly as if they were

Dead lovers waiting
For numbered immortality.

We crawl to cellars to rescue them
From plastic oblivion,

Above us the autumn world
Of rusting leaves

And sick bus-tickets
Salting this season's gutter.

SIGNING HIM AWAY

.'For eighteen years I waited for his call,
And when it came
I feared his voice. I heard the same brutal
Seduction, the same
Dark timbre. Double pain.

And I'd be lacking all the qualities
Surrounding him:
No clever turn of phrase, no sparkling speech
To wallpaper my shame,
No childhood clichés.

No day without a thought for him, always
Regret at signing
Him away. Oh, but his eyes
Would burn and sting,
Would sue my dreams,

Would claim his other life, and mine.
I sit here trembling
Waiting for his face, not knowing
How to mime the mother role, dreading
His footfall and the ring

I cannot answer.'

KNOWLEDGE

Always
I am the serpent
For his dark strength,

Always
I am the small child
Slipping into his green silk,

Always
The dust between my toes
On the way to his house.

CASSANDRA IN MYCENAE

Apollo chose me,
Held me coiled inside his hand
And yet I would not yield to him.

And though I broke
Through sense and reason
In distress with all the destined

Horror that I saw
And no one would believe my words
I still remain his tool, his priestess.

Not even Priam,
King and father, heeded my prophesy,
He plunged me in that beehive prison tomb

Where few survive.
All this I had to bear
Alone—far from myself—and loss of Troy.

Now sold and exiled
With my enemy's return
I still must see and warn

And fear to enter
Agamemnon's gate
Where Clytemnestra's shadow waits.

Oh darkness that condemns
My life, smother my eyes
And so release me from this gift,

Take me to sisters' caves
To whiteness on Mount Ida,
The pain will stay behind.

WHITE MORNING

There is a white sunrise
Lightening through mist,
Making the day larger,
More autumnal.

Acid leaves are falling;
And the round pain,
Too, falls on sunlight
Like red apples blinding the ground.

A SHORT DIRGE FOR SONIA

When I was pregnant
I read the Russians,

And if you were female
I'd call you Sonia:

Raskolnikov's girl
Who was loyal and cheap,

A prostitute saint.
She knelt in my dreams.

But I had a son
and could never test

Or pursue that allusion
In furthest Siberia

To find my own daughter.

PIETA (for Katharine)

She will always go to him,
There, on the hill's elbow,
Feeling his purity
Rejecting man's compromise.

She will bring him flowers
And words of glass
Running with her tears.

She will tell her grief
To the wild grasses,
Her hands unsteady
From his ruined birth,
His youth falling
From the Friday of love
And the mind's passion.

Then, touching the earth,
She will hold the brief joy
Of his life in her arms
Trying to understand death.

POST MORTEM

I met her in the market on the day
Her dog had died. And she, so shy and sparse
Of speech at other times, spilled grief among

The cabbages. "He must have had a heart
Condition and we never realized,
We smacked and scolded him for muddy paws

When he came in, and then he just collapsed!
We blame ourselves, we should have coddled him."
And so she fluttered on in her distress:

"There'll be an autopsy, we have to know."
Then she begged pardon for her riot words
And hid behind the burden of her eyes.

OCTOBER POEM

Time of sugar-beet burning
In this adopted town
Where curls of smoke dance
Or hang in a clear sky,
The fierce October light
Warming the auburn day.

This, my birth month, begins
To collect early nights,
Writes accounts of glass-cut years,
Pays out memories that salt,
Sweeten, sour the future,
Sends the bill to mankind.

THE GREEN PLEASURE

There is this green pleasure
Of shelling the first peas—
The gentle thumb-press
At the top till they split open
Revealing those small pearls
Sweet and crisp for quick cooking.

Each summer I look forward
To their lips parting
With a mild pop, air escaping
From the still young pods
And watch the pot filling
With each green promise.

FIRE BLIGHT

That tree stood in its parchment death
For a year
Not losing a branch or a leaf,
No clear
Sign of any sickness at first.
Only colour
Was fading slowly, unexpectedly
From its trunk
And later the leaves accepted
A locked
Greyness that deepened as the months passed.
Even in spring
It held on to that sackcloth appearance.
Fire-blight:
A strange attack on unseen
Devils
Riding the atmosphere, radiating
Invisible
Poison onto this old giant
So that he stood
Bloodless and burnt while we watched.

JULY JOURNEY

Driving through torn, molested countryside
To someone's wedding day, we see the poppies
Rioting on clumps of upturned earth
As if they'd fling their brief exuberance
Against the sky before their season dies.

Clouds, that surround us like a ring of white-
Gowned nuns, their vigil gentled by the wind,
Grow taller with each mile so as to hide
The blueness underneath their spreading arms,
Their habits greying with the ageing day.

And where the blessings crumble from the lips
Of priests, a congregation joins in rites of tongues
Defying rutted earth and faceless clouds.
We travel with our backs against the sky
Daring to meet it in a half-way house.

THOUGHT SHAPES

The inky shape
Walking ahead of me,
Stretched flat across the path,

I trust I know her well.
Her skin contains all
That I feel and think.

But like that bird above
In the new April tree,
A hovering otherness

Issues another world,
And unmet thoughts
Reject that speeding shape.

IN PRAISE OF SILENCE

In the glass coffin lies the Ayatollah,
Students are crushed and burnt in Peking square.
We sit in front of all that TV horror
And massage our rheumatic knees with care.

The telephone demands another section
Of the short day. A voice defends the word,
The long elastic of communication
So vital when the island sound is feared.

Yet we must listen to the silent language
Inside the grass blade, stone, record the tree.
Remember presences that work their magic
Only in solitude—for none to see.

IV

WHEN THE CLOCKS

When the clocks tick as near
as if they lived in your own heart
and things grow timid and start
to question the thought:
Are you here?

Then I'm not the one who each morning awakes;
night gives me a name that no one takes,
that no one I spoke with during the day
could have experienced without deep fear—

and every door
in me gives way . . .

And then I know nothing has passed,
no gesture, no prayer is lost

(because the things have too much weight)
all my childhood is constantly
standing about my fate.
I am never alone.
Many who've lived before me
were striving away from me
weaving
weaving
my being, my own.

And shall I sit down near you
and quietly say: I have suffered—
do you hear?
    Who knows who
    will murmur it too.

                  (after Rainer Maria Rilke)

AUTUMN DAY

Lord: it is time. The summer was so great.
Lay down your shadow on the sundial's face
and in the meadows let the winds run riot.

Command the last fruits fullness in this time;
present them still with two more southern days
to urge them to perfection and to chase
the final sweetness into heavy wine.

Who has no house now, will not build his own.
Who is alone now, long will stay the same,
will sit up late, read, write long letters, roam
restlessly through tree-lined streets, again
walk back and forth when leaves ride in the storm.

(after Rainer Maria Rilke)

SONNET TO ORPHEUS IX

Only he, whose lyre was raised
even among shadows,
dare sing the unending praise
his sense barely knows.

Only he, who ate their meal
of poppy-seed with the dead,
will not lose the softest peal
of tone and thread.

If the pond's mirror often
for us may get blurred:
The image stays.

In the twofold sphere alone
shall voices be heard:
Mild and always.

(after Rainer Maria Rilke)

LOTUS FLOWER (for Mouche)

Truly, we are both making
A very curious pair,
The beloved weak on her legs,
The lover lame in her care.

She is a kitten that's ailing
And he a dog that is sick;
I think both their heads are playing
A most unhealthy trick.

She would be a lotus flower,
So the darling fancies her scene;
Yet he, the pale, poor fellow,
Imagines himself as the moon.

In moonlight the lotus flower
Unlocks her little throat,
But instead of the pollen of life
A poem her only reward.

(after Heinrich Heine)

NIGHT RAIN

Rain's equanimity! A dead roar!
The more you try, the more you listen,
The less of substance you will hear.

Intensity won't lose your world.
The dull rain stammers senselessly.
You can't extort one word from God.

Give up your greediness, your grasping!
The one who waits receives no song,
But let surprise completeness bring.

(after Franz Werfel)